A funny way with words

ROB STEPNEY
JOHN LANYON
ADRIAN LANCINI
EDWARD FENTON

THE WYCHWOOD PRESS

Our books may be ordered from
bookshops or (post free) from
The Wychwood Press, Alder House,
Market Street, Charlbury, OX7 3PH
01608 819117
e-mail: orders@wychwoodpress.co.uk

First published in 2012 by
The Wychwood Press
an imprint of Jon Carpenter Publishing
Alder House, Market Street, Charlbury,
Oxfordshire OX7 3PH

ISBN 978 1 902279 48 0

Design and illustration by Adrian Lancini

Printed in England by
CPI Antony Rowe Ltd.,
Chippenham SN14 6LH

No seahorses were harmed
in the making of this book

An A to 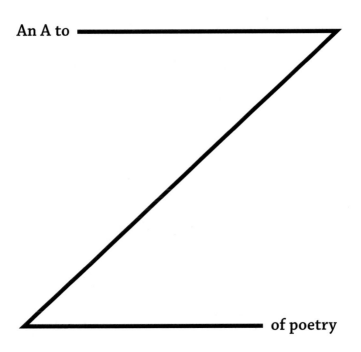 of poetry

A is for April, 'the cruellest month', before

Bs are properly buzzing.

C is in Charlbury, though we're miles from the shore.

D's for decay, which we hope's long in coming.

E for emotion.

F could be effing, and blinding too. But perhaps

G is for genial, and

H for honest – not that

I am the subject.

J for joyful wagging of a

K nine tail.

L for Eliot.

M for metre.

N for end, which is

Omega too.

P is a problem if you're stuck in a

Q.

R for rhyme.

S for essence.

T for two and

U for me.

V for Victory, and if I

Double you that would be

X for unknown. But surely

Y is for wine leading to

Zed zed zed for bed.

AS A LAD I WAS CLUMSY, all fingers and thumbs,
My teachers would hit me with rulers.
When they told me to 'Listen!',
I said 'I'm all ears' –
Now I spend all my time at the jeweller's.

Then when I had run out of room on my ears
I went back to my jeweller
to have my heart pierced.

Now I think that I love her,
but where do I start?
Butterflies in my stomach,
and holes in my heart.

Pierced

The first day of spring

How arrogant of us
To bequeath a date
For spring's arrival
How dare we!

Spring is to be sprung
Like a kiss to the lips
When we lunge for a cheek

The daffodil consults no diary
It consults the earth
The sun
The air
And perhaps, the bumble bee.

DANGEROUS outside *leaning*

Written, in my native language of Esperanto,
in a sleeping compartment on the 20.30 from
Munich to Florence. The train arrived nine
hours later and two minutes early.

A rectangular bed

in a small square box,

In a carriage that's a clickety can
Clickety can Clickety can Clickety can...

Almost a prison
Except the guard says 'Lock yourself from the inside'

If I don't do that
Who might I meet?

Better bolt myself tight with my musings

So the door stays firmly
'Fermé, Zu, Chiuso, Shut'

One small cell with
Five sets of prohibitions on the walls
(Like Leviticus on wheels)

L'usage du cabinet WC
Est interdit
In stations
(Lest those working underneath
Get it in the eyes and teeth,
And that would sorely try their patience)

On the wall a socket

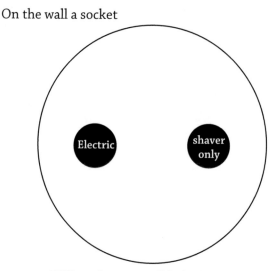

Will not be responsible for improper use

(Haven't you always wanted to use an electric
shaver improperly?)

From the menu I order a '**spuntino freddo serale***'
(Daring, since nothing tells me
What the asterisk may mean)

The light evening dinner comes with an arancia drink
(Because you're not allowed water from the sink)
A drink con vitamino, calcio,
e fosforo

For those who want a light

But rauchen is verboten in the
compartamiento overnight

On the window

E' pericoloso sporgersi

(Goodness, don't you sometimes long to sporgersi?)

'Nicht hinauslehnen!'

 For any Dummkopf riding for a fall

  But better pay attencion

   Since, sans Kopf, is no arrival at all.

The old doors
Made by hand
Open the past.

from: HAIKU TEA

Walking
the
dog
in
winter

Fallen snow, one tenth water
and nine tenths light

The brown earth already bears

A heavy weight of white

The sky's so promising with
further blizzard

It's almost black

For added emphasis,

Each dark branch is thickly
overlaid with icing

Against the fallen snow,

Our black and white dog's
ruff is cream

And his name is 'Blue'.

METHYL
MERCAPTAN
WHAT
ARE YOU

Methyl Mercaptan – what are you?

Are you a forgotten Welsh fishing port?

Or a drug made from blubber to inject, smoke or snort?

Methyl Mercaptan – what are you?

Are you a laid back greeting used by Rastafarians?

Or a brand of vodka, guzzled by Hungarians?

Methyl Mercaptan – what are you?
Are you a mythical creature?
Half meerkat, half orangutan, with wings
From Jason and the Argonauts or Lord of the Rings?

Methyl Mercaptan – what are you?
Are you 'chewing gum' in Norwegian?
Eskimo for 'Not now, Stephen'?
A captain of the Foreign Legion?
A cow, but not a Friesian?

Methyl Mercaptan – what are you?
Are you the white spirit
Pablo Picasso used to wash his brushes clean?
Or are you the Citroen Picasso's
Recommended wash for the screen?

Methyl Mercaptan – what are you?
Are you a Northern Indian dish,
Pan-fried mutton, chilli and mint?
Or something the Vikings said
When they were totally skint?

Methyl Mercaptan – I know what you are!
You are the pungent gas that's ever-surprisingly unleashed
Urinating 15 minutes after dinner
When asparagus was in the quiche.

They drive you mad

The curtains

the former Mrs made

25 years ago,

Thin and unlined, beige,

A little too large,

Some of the rings broken,

Still hanging around,

After all these years

They wake you early,

Pale and translucent

Not quite worn out

Something from

an old drama

From a theatre that closed

You go

I deserve better than this

I go

They're just curtains, OK?

Once they were 100% cotton,

Once the fabric came from Habitat

curt

ains

You're like
I want luxury,
I want softness,
I want darkness.
Just buy some!
I'm like
Just show me the man
Who chose his own curtains.

An unprimed canvas
For a picture unpainted.
Dust sheets,
Improvised bandages,
Escape from a locked room,
Sailcloth from the *Victory*,
A screen for shadow puppets.

I could go on
But I realise
(It's taken a while)
I've had enough of symbols.
It's time to learn about colour,
To find a pattern that fits.

Browing old gracefully

There comes a time
when eyebrow tufts grow at

●

an unsettling angle to the rest

And you must settle to
a life of Dennis Healey

●

Coming Out

Last night Matthew
Manors slept soundly

The night before that
he had come out.
Both parents were proud

The night before that
he'd decided breasts
just weren't for him

The night before that
he had cried and cried
and cried

And the night before
that, he was born.

The Towns
and Villages of
OXFORDSHIRE

YOU WOULD NOT BELIEVE the lengths I have to go to get
my books stocked in Tom Joyner's bookshop, here in town.

You see, I've just produced a book of stories about the
towns and villages of Oxfordshire. So I went to him and
said: 'COMBE on ... Won't you take just one or TEW ?'

And you know what he told me? 'There isn't exactly a
WANTAGE for that sort of thing.' He's got a funny way
with words ...

I was gobsmacked. 'You're KIDDINGTON ... I mean,
you're kidding, Tom.' But he wouldn't listen. And in the
end I just told him. 'You and me, mate – we're heading
for a showdown. Just like in some spaghetti WESTON
ON THE GREEN !"

22

Now, Tom has a routine. 1 o'clock each day he leaves his shop and heads down to Sheep Street, [FAWLER] his afternoon snacks.

I looked at my watch. 'If I'm [GAGINGWELL], I've got 10 minutes ... '

I ran back home, got a trestle table and a load of books – they must've weighed [ENSTONE]! – and went back down, to [LYNEHAM] up outside the Charlbury Deli.

Next I had to round up some of the local layabouts ... Where were you? Instead I found a bunch of kids playing [HOOKY] – from school, you know.

I went up to their ringleader ... 'Okay, here's the plan: [ISLIP] you a fiver – you come down and "buy" some of my books ... Show a certain person they're a [OTMOOR] popular than he thinks they are!'

He stared at me. 'What's that, [BICESTER]?' – I think he had sinus problems ... 'A fiver's of [LITTLEWORTH]. Twenty, and it's a deal!'

'Done! Round up your mates, and [MARCHAM] down there – I'll see you there in one minute!' And I ran on ahead, just in time to see Tom Joyner, [HEADINGTON] the Charlbury Deli. Yes!

But where were the kids? Five whole minutes later they rolled up, with my 20 quid, and disappeared into News and Things to buy a [POUNDON] a half of every sweet in the shop.

I rapped on the window. 'Hey! What about my books?'
The ringleader half-opened the door. 'Books? [GORING]!'
'But you know [FULWELL] – you promised!'
'[ARDLEY]!'
'Then I'll have my money back!'
And that's when the air turned blue. Suddenly
everything was [BLENHEIM] this, and [BLADON] that ...
It was enough to make Ozzy Osbourne sound [THAME].
And just then Tom Joyner came out of the Deli –
he had a [GREAT ROLLRIGHT], in one hand – and he was
singing! '[SUMMERTOWN] and the living is easy ... '
He [DIDCOT] even look at me. I felt a proper [CHARLBURY].
But I always like to look on the [BRIGHTWELL] side –
and [WATERPERRY] good idea it's given me! I'm going
to write up what happened, and it'll be the first story
in 'A Book of Stories about the Towns and Villages of
Oxfordshire', volume 2! It'll be [BRILL].
And now surely, Tom Joyner [WOODSTOCK] that.

I've got seven suits
In seven shades of grey
I've got people who tell me
What I've got to say
I've got more froth
I've got more spin
Than the cappuccino world
I like dipping in
They all say Hey, Joe...
I dig your braggadocio

BRAGGADOCIO

Braggadocio ...
That's the mojo
That lets you in the dojo
Braggadocio ...
Hear me on a talk show
A cup of tea?
Does that fit my beverage portfolio?
Braggadocio ...
I'll get back to you on that one.
Let me run that by you
One more time ...

Braggadocio.

The Middle of Nowhere

I found myself in the Middle of Nowhere. I hadn't even noticed the sign for Nowhere but there I found myself, in the middle of it. I took a photo of it on my phone and returned to Somewhere.

On my return I told someone I'd been to the Middle of Nowhere but they didn't believe me. They said 'Well, you must have been somewhere!' So I got out my phone and showed them the photograph I'd taken.

They said I could have photoshopped it and taken everything out. But my phone is a 2002 model Nokia 7650, which, as everyone knows, has no photo editing facilities. Proof beyond reasonable and unreasonable doubt that I had, indeed, been to the Middle of Nowhere.

Fame and fortune quickly followed. Everybody wanted to hear my story – *National Geographic*, Buckingham Palace, the Jonathan Ross Show. I'd gone from the Middle of Nowhere to being Everywhere.

Elsewhere, Hollywood to be exact, a film was to be made about me. Johnny Depp and Gérard Depardieu were in the running to play my role. Hollywood couldn't decide between them so they asked me, 'Depp or Depardieu?'

I couldn't decide either. I mean, Depp's got my looks but Depardieu's got my .... timing.

I received letters from both actors imploring me to choose them. The pressure was getting to me. But worse was to follow.

Other letters. Malicious ones. From people all over the world claiming to have been to the Middle of Nowhere themselves.

I even received death threats, and one package that contained a kettle, an out-of-date Pot Noodle and a bottle of water that turned out to be hydrogen cyanide.

Under the strain I just had to get away. I was desperate to escape from the world. There was only one thing for it – I returned to the Middle of Nowhere. For good. I became a nobody, doing nothing nowhere.

If you ever find yourself in the Middle of Nowhere my advice would be – keep it to yourself. You just don't know where the Middle of Nowhere could lead.

WHEN MIGHT TIME HAVE

After radio but before TV
Post the (PILL) but pre HIV

Let's have the **fax** but not the mobile phone
Last orders, but not the long walk home

Before Altamont, but after Woodstock
Post Doctor Who but pre Doctor Spock

When grass was greener, before hydroponic skunk
Pre New Romantics but post Sid Vicious **Punk**

Before Modern Art – and Never Mind the Pollocks

Après garlic but avant nouvelle cuisine
Between the then and the might have been

STOPPED?

When a cheese is poised between ripeness and rot
Just before your spoon enters the honey pot

In the crisp hours before slush follows snow
When you know you must part but before you must go

Between an inspiration and its ~~edits~~
The climax and the credits

Or between the credit and the Crunch

Between the future and the past
The first breath and the last

Between the *rush* of revolution
And the onset of reality

Post World War II but pre World War III.

I WANT

to save this, moon lodged
in a tree, Above the golden cropped
cornfield, above the town. I want to share
the sunset here in peace, And make a standing
circle with my words, To remember it by. Here in
the twilight, Birds greet the dawning of another night.

And when the quiet sun has slipped away
Leaving the summer colours smudged like oils
The streets and the rooftops disappear
In the woodsmoke and trees, soon fading too.
And on the horizon, a single car
Shines its headlights like the evening star.

A **good** soldier

Tales of you walking in the high hills
Of Kashmir and Kilimanjaro,
Trading jewels in the market place
Riding in your armoured-car
across the desert,
Fixing the engine in the dark,
Capturing the proudest tribesmen
With your battered Leica,
Catching huge silver-bellied fish
by the lakeside,
Exchanging words in Hindi,
Punjabi, Arabic and Swahili;

7883943 Sergeant Lanyon

I salute you and ask
What strategy decided
That you would die, without grammar,
In your wheelchair tank
From some mysterious internal war.

It's a mistake
to look in

THE MIRROR

A thickening of the waist

A brow neatly furrowed

But there are championships in ploughing.

Dear Hazel I'm sorry that Whoeveritwas you gave the book to
didn't
like it
enough
to keep
it
but a
dark
tale
with
sadistic
overtones
doesn't
seem the
obvious
way
to cement
a friendship.
That you
didn't
write a
name, or
Dear, or
Darling
suggests
haste

Happy Birthday
Love from Hazel.

But you gave with love which somehow insists on living.

Arising from the Ashes

(Edgbaston 2005)

Phlegmatic Vaughan fired Flintoff
And, when flints spark, even age-cold Ashes catch alight.
The hairy Hoggard showed his well-timed flair,
Strauss waltzed the wicket
And Bell peeled catches from short-leg mid-air

Once misdescribed as King of Spain,
Ace spinbowler Giles
Put the typo to the Test.
He dipped and weaved with all the wiles
Of Spain's ballfighters at their best.

Pietersen, more bear than Boer with bat,
Belted planets out of battered leather
While Jones the gloves and Jones the ball
Sang in Harmison with it all.
And the latter's slow one-fingered fling
Contrived the crucial wicket's fall.

Edgbaston: the first and best and closest victory

Later, at Trent Bridge, that risky run.
Too little clout.
'Howzat?' asked England, and the answer's 'Out'.
No racing heartbeat of a doubt
The Aussie captain was caught short.
Ponting's ensuing tantrum tires.
But there's no true bloke without ire.

In batting, tall Trescothick stood his ground,
Though Man of Corn he be,
Unbending in the storm of wild McGrath
And even of Brett Lee.
Despite the guts and balls of Warne,
From Oz the Ashes fairly shorn,
And all Downunder mourn.

A definition of entropy that's true,
if difficult to express in maths:

The force of children at work in the universe

No thing or feeling will ever be in its accustomed place

B   E   Y   O   N   D
Newton's laws

If I love you a million, it's seven letters

And seven figures, and two syllables, or maybe three;

But if I love you to the top of the stars, it's infinity

L^{Our}ocal

The good ship Rose, harboured in our town
A vessel within a vessel, here be found

To travel from ale to ale, without destination
To travel on laughter and fine conversation

Hours are killed before our very eyes
Murder a pint
Shoot down a bloody Mary
Finish off a wine
And before you know it, the cruellest act of all
Closing time

So good ship Rose, sail on and on and on and on

Like Ariston
the advert from the early 80s.

The other day I was in the bank
My whole life flashed before my eyes
When the queue of people standing there
Was joined by four men in disguise
Waving guns above our head
One move, they said, and we'd be dead

We're armed, dangerous men
Armed and dangerous men

Well, two of them stood by the door
And made us get down on the floor
The other two rushed to the counter
Rifles cocked for their encounter
It can't have been their lucky day
Because all the staff had run away
I shan't repeat what I heard them say
When they saw the staff had run away

They were armed, dangerous men
Armed and dangerous men

Well the doors were solid, windows too
They didn't know quite what to do
That's when they started shouting loud
And turned their guns upon the crowd
They shouted 'Hurry, don't be funny
Come on and give us all your money!'

We're armed, dangerous men
Armed and dangerous men

One poor bloke began to cry
He said 'Here's five quid, I don't want to die'
But I hadn't come to put money in
I was there to take some money out
So what could I give them, what could I do
When the men with guns began to shout

We're armed, dangerous men
Armed and dangerous men

And as I lay there in a sweat
I thought about the night we met
We'd been sitting side by side
On the way to Oxford on the Park and Ride
You were talking about some band
You wrote your number on my hand
Then as we headed off down the street
Our ears were greeted by the garage beat
Passers-by were asking 'what's that din?'
As we went upstairs and walked straight in

It's party time, we're having fun
It's party time, we're having fun

I don't know if they were breaking the law
But they'd broken the ice, and then some more
I must admit it was quite a sight
All those flashing legs and flashing lights
Soon our bodies were moving to the pulsing sound
When suddenly the doors came crashing down
And twenty policemen came rushing in –
Just like in the bank, here they were again.
With a 'Drop your guns, or else we'll fire'
They put the robbers in the Black Maria

They were armed, dangerous men
Armed and dangerous men

But they didn't even take my name
Never asked for a statement about the crime
And I've just seen two paragraphs
On page 17 of the *Oxford Times*
It says they're cracking down on illegal raves:
'The men behind them must be stopped.'
But due to a technicality
The robbers have had all charges dropped.

So forget about those men with guns –
Seems the dangerous thing is having fun.

I don't want to seem picky

But why not **ask**
For the **perfect** life
The perfect **death**
And the perfect
resurrection?

Her thick coat of grass -
She left it off all winter
Like a strong-willed child.

+

Snow: Christmas in a Quaker meeting house

If God had not given us snow for fun

WOULD MAN HAVE MADE IT?

Or made it, and packed it, and sold it?

OR MADE IT, AND PACKED IT, AND SOLD IT

and used it as a material of war?

The Dos and Don'ts of Leaving-dos

Dos

Bring along replacements for every item you have stolen from the stationery cupboard. Yes, even that 4H pencil. The guilt may not be affecting you right now but it will doubtlessly haunt you on your death bed.

Say you will try to keep in touch with everybody, even though it's glaringly obvious to all that you'll never want to contact Simon Mulland from Accounts ever again.

Offer to buy a round of drinks. You've been working with these guys for quite some time. Don't be tight and leave them with a bitter taste in their mouths – unless of course their favourite tipple happens to be bitter.

Order the crab. Make sure you remember to bring your last works contract with you. When the crab arrives place it on your contract, turn to your boss and say 'I don't remember seeing the claws in my contract before.' Everyone will laugh.

Have a plan in place for a friend to phone with a watertight excuse for you to suddenly leave, in the event of Karen Deveaux insisting you should all move on to Krystals Nightclub half-price Tia Maria night.

Don'ts

Don't call in sick. No one will believe you – just like they didn't believe you all the other times you called in sick – even on that day when you were actually physically sick on the phone when calling in sick.

Don't get too downhearted when a colleague you've seen nearly every day for seven years merely writes *'All the best'* in your leaving card.

Don't excuse yourself for the toilet and then announce you are going for a pee 45. No one will laugh.

Don't sing. They'll want you to. Oh, how they'll want you to, but don't. Even when you've had three Camparis try to resist singing at all costs. Simon Mulland will be poised with his camera and will post a movie of your performance on YouTube, under the title '#KNOB HEAD ALERT LOL '.

Don't be disappointed if you receive a £30 voucher for British Home Stores as a leaving gift. It may seem like pittance for giving seven years of your life but BHS are currently doing a classic six-item breakfast for £3*, which means you can have ten slap-up breakfasts for nothing.

*Oxford branch, Sept 2012

BAD THINGS WERE DONE IN EPHESUS

It wasn't like meeting the ghost of Pliny or St Paul,
Though both men when alive had walked these streets.
But it was an odd encounter, at the ruins' edge,
An old man with a bucket, on top of which were fig leaves.
They covered an embarrassment of snails.
To eat, he gestured.

I knew the word for 'greens',
And mimed a gardener's displeasure at what snails ate.

We matched well in the matter of moustaches.
(His perhaps a little grizzlier.)
But his apparent taste for snails, and my distaste,
Seemed a natural limit to communication.
Then he undid a knotted handkerchief.
Inside, a ring with bearded head,
Delicately carved, in reverse relief.

This time he spoke: 'I sell to eat. Good price for you.'
From walks along the Evenlode,
I knew the snails weren't Roman.
Nor, almost certainly, the ring.

Caveat emptor. For a wealth of reasons.

But what if it had been real, and I had bought it,
To save a man from eating snails, or out of avarice?
Worse things were done in Ephesus.

There was someone – it may even have been me –
Who dared disturb a brick, and with his own hand
Trace the maker's fingers as they formed
the snakelike swirl
That keyed it to the mortar in antiquity.

The night of Alexander's birth, a madman torched
the temple of Artemis,
Then the seventh wonder of the world.
Not only the dictator Syrpax, but all his family
Were stoned to death.
And bones found outside the walls of Ephesus
Show what it took to meet the appetite
for bread and circuses.

One man fighting for his life, but others' entertainment
Was brought low, his knee smashed
By a weapon like a four-pronged knitting needle
Designed precisely for this purpose,
And a feature of the games in Ephesus.

Another's skull was neatly holed by
two prongs of a trident.
A third had a problem with his back.
Not a slipped disc, you understand.
More a sword thrust from behind
That sheared two vertebrae
And then neatly sliced his heart.
The odds of dying in this trade's first season
Were two in three.

Caveat gladiator. For a range of reasons.

According to the city's famed philosopher, one Heraclitus,
Everything is flowing.
Perhaps because he'd seen much blood.
Bad things were done in Ephesus.

BAD
MIN
TON

You are like a flower, attentive to the sky;
Or clock, ticking your head as the shuttlecock tocks by.
How did we ever have a child so beautiful?

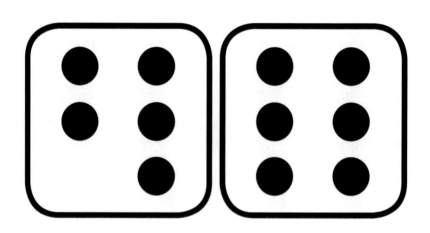

Swag belly

Swagbelly drives a Robin Reliant
He never took no test and she's startin' to sway
Head down, white knuckles
He's suckin' sweets on the big highway

Don't knock me down, Mr Swagbelly
Don't knock me down

He don't worry about bumps and scratches
The clutch and the gearbox are leaking oil
Fags in the ashtray, foot on the floor
Cracks in the block and she's beginning to boil

Don't knock me down, Mr Swagbelly
Don't knock me down

No maps, no signs, no exits, no hassles
Fluorescent seat covers and a family of mice
Departure, arrival, freedom, survival –
It's all in the roll of the big furry dice

Don't knock me down, Mr Swagbelly
Don't knock me down.

The man who wouldn't poo until he got to work so he never had to buy toilet paper

Tight arse.

Gobble Devon Dumpling

Words go on holiday and are seen in some most unfamiliar places.
Written to celebrate the brews available at the 2011 Charlbury
Beer Festival (motto: Walk In and Hop Out).

Gobble Devon Dumpling, all English Doff Cocker
Eton Amber Bakewell and Chocolate Orange Stout
Glossop great Cheddar, Oak ham,
And Wild Boar washed down with BG Sips

Or, forsaking Inndulgence,
Dinting Arches and All Black Deception,
Rail ale. Break Water!
Sleck Dust and
Wandle Mild and Gluten Free
(Even if Uffington
O'er Shropshire Summerhill)
Through Mersey Mist and Fenny Pocket
Harvest Pennine Gold
Be at Gorge Best, Teignworthy
Windsor, Conqueror, Victory
And Crack Shot.

LET'S
HEAR IT
FOR THE
WEIRD
KID

Jazz in a brown jumper,

You look so vulnerable,

The kind of jumper

Your mum might buy you,

Thin and commonplace,

Warm enough
for a new sound?

A woolly jumper
hugs you close,

A plastic saxophone,
you hug it close,

A ghost of a smile
on your face.

HYPOTHETICAL TRIBUTE ACTS – A TOP 40

1. Not Chocolate
2. Rob Dylan
3. Irony Maiden
4. Dis ain't Rascal
5. The Scousemartins
6. Vanessa Parody
7. Tonight Alan is Morissette
8. Phoney M
9. Paul McCan't Be
10. Shoddywaddy
11. Johnny Cash-in
12. Just ain't Timberlake
13. Mock The Hoople
14. Theftfield
15. Blag Sabbath
16. Mimic Hucknall
17. Jenny's Sis
18. Adam Aren't
19. S Pub 7
20. Paul Karaokenfold
21. The Isley Others
22. MC Stammer
23. Quite Said Fred
24. Replicate Bush
25. Busker Rhymes
26. Neo Sayer
27. Aretha Skankin
28. Frifty Cent
29. Sample Minds
30. It's no Patrol
31. The Wonderbluff
32. Tributsey Collins
33. Otis Wedding
34. Gloria It's a Fan
35. Boy Forge
36. Rick Ghastly
37. Paul Well I Never
38. I Can't Believe It's Not Bernard Butler
39. Musical Spoof
40. Bucks Swizz

Praise be to Jason King and Dr Ben Gurney-Smith for their part in compiling this.

The miracle of flight

Seeking portents, people for centuries have scanned the sky.

Tonight, miles above Milan, there is a perfect cross.

'The Last Supper', by Leonardo, lies immediately below.

Lonely souls, da Vinci and Jesus both

Contemplated flight, through air or desert.

But what would they have made of millions flying?

The mystification of stagnant vapour trails, Chalk-mark condensations,

Compared with a bird free
to move with no trace

Except for the fixated eyes
of two cats on the roof

Hungry, and desperate
for wings.

harpooning HARPOONING HARPOONING HARPOONING HAI

Far from the ocean, no whales in sight
You know that the desert gets so cold at night
With a crescent moon casting a pale silhouette
Against the wall of the old minaret
I heard a strange noise, then shortly after
The haunting sound of girls' laughter.

When I saw her standing there
With her deep dark eyes and her long dark hair
A sultry smile as wide as the Nile
My cold English heart started falling apart
And the stars were shining like diamonds above me
As she turned and told me she loved me.

Well after one minute or maybe two
She'd used up all of the words she knew
She barely knew more than two or three
Just enough to tell me she loved me.

HARPOONING HARPOO

I said I had to meet a friend
But I hoped that we could meet again
The next night I waited for the girl I had dated
I was washed up all night, she was nowhere in sight
And the stars still shining like diamonds above me
But no one to tell me they loved me.

My friend just laughed, he said she'd been fooling
He told me the local kids called it 'harpooning'
Their idea of a joke, harpooning some bloke.

HARPOONING HARPOONING HARPOONING HARPOONING HARPOONING HARPOONING HARPOONING HARPOONING HARPOONING HARPOONING HARPOONING HARPOONING HARPOONING HARPOONING ►

My poor heart was yearning, my stomach was churning –
What set my heart burning, the loss of my love
Or the sun like an A-bomb above?

'There's plenty more fish in the sea,' said my man
As we trekked across the desert sand
But of all the girls in the whole wide world
Of all the girls, if I had my pick
I'd pick that girl, the harpoon girl
Who made me Moby Dick.

Who's the stranger

At table 7?

The guy with the ghosts

That ain't going to Heaven.

He said Put it on the Red

Put it on the Black

It doesn't matter anyhow

'Cos it ain't coming back.

I've stuck, I've twisted

I'm flushed, I'm busted

And I want to play again

And I want to play again.

CASINO OF LOVE

60

CASINO OF LOVE

She said I'm the Queen

And you're the Jack

Looking at what you got

I can beat that

Lost you in a card game

Been messin' with the pack

Going to be a King

Going to win you back

I've stuck, I've twisted

I'm flushed, I'm busted

And I want to play again

And I want to play again

61

Not Adam's Apple

This is the long-awaited week.
The one week in the year,
When the window of the gabled room
In which I strive to write
Fills with apple blossom.

It clumps on branches
Like wet, late-fallen snow
Rimmed with the pink of a dawning sun.
If every flower produced a heavy fruit,
The world would surely overturn.

The tree itself is old, perhaps has the canker.
Its forks grow moss.
Each year a few more branches fail to flower.
The autumn apples are small,
Misshapen, sometimes bitter,
Each with its own earwig,
And would never have tempted Adam.

But this tree has outlived
The purposes of procreation,
Nutrition and temptation.
It flowers now only to crown the rites
Of these seven sacred days of spring.

Lesser spotted doxy

A taxi lets go a girl

Who lopes off tightly leopard-arsed
down Lime Street

Looking so much at home

My genes too were here

But respectable Welsh

Minding their manners

And never ones to flaunt the skin
of an exotic animal

Even in facsimile

For the purpose of provocation.

Liverpool, 2012

Touchstone

Oh, my Archaeologist,
We can't go on meeting like this,
Leaving a rusty Ford Escort, Diamond White,
To step lightly at dusk
Into le domaine mystérieux,
Walking beyond le château familial
On lush grass and rain-washed gravel
Through avenues of pear trees.
We meet the white horse from your childhood,
Glimpse the friendly lights in the gardener's cottage.
I search the night air for the scent of jasmine.
I cannot find it.

Oh, my Archaeologist,
We can't go on meeting like this
Another time against a vicious
Landscape of stone,
Wind-hacked and storm-carved.
This defiant stone is my ancestor,
Rising, crusted with lichen, from the headland.
Lift it to your lips,
Trace the lines of the lode,
Find me in it.

Oh, my Archaeologist, it's History!
There is no definitive landscape
I create them for you
Because you smile beautifully.
For you I fight
Conventional Romantic Symbols
With a tight-lipped irony.

Fog.
Fog from the Atlantic
Envelops my stone.
Fog. A final
impenetrable symbol.
There is no clear way
into history.

Oh, my Archaeologist,
We can't go on meeting like this
Except perhaps in some sheltered spot
Where the scented jasmine might
Grow among the furze.
I do not know such a place,
But I can make it for you.

Fourteen websites that don't actually exist* no t

www.shinsure.com
The only place on the internet offering low cost insurance for people's shins.

www.loveclingfilm.com
Unlimited cling film posted to your door for £7.99 a month. When you've used it all send the empty tube back in the FREEPOST envelope provided. They'll cover it back over with cling film and post it back.

www.bedtimetory.com
Conservative MPs of the past and present read children's books out loud. Edwina Currie does *The Witches*. William Hague does *The Gruffalo*.

www.thewineseller.com
Buy wine on the internet! Entrepreneur David Petantahook explains 'Many people who have internet access also like wine. I simply married the two together.' David says a lot of people get confused about the name when they hear it. 'It's ambiguous when it's said because it could mean seller as in selling or cellar as in the place wine is traditionally stored!' he mumbled.

*yet.

com

www.thornographic.com
Members only adult site for people who are aroused by the Hawthorn tree. A prickly topic indeed. An angry Mrs Ivy Moss from the Barking branch of the Anti-Thornographic League remarked 'They should leaf it out. It's just knot on. They wood probably say I'm an old fruit but this filth gives me the creepers. It will sap all my energy but I aim to root these people out and nip this in the bud. Do you twig?'

www.anglosalon.com
The official website for 'Anglo Salon' – a chain of hairdressing salons specialising in ancient hairdos.

www.comeonbabyinflatemytyre.com
Car MOT, servicing and breakdown cover exclusively for people believing themselves to be the reincarnation of Jim Morrison.

www.harrisinparis.com
Watch movies online of Rolf Harris in the French capital painting from blanc canvas to finished pieces. 'Vous avez déjà reconnu ce que c'est?'

www.bryanair.com

Buy sealed bags of air breathed into by famous Bryans. Bags include air breathed by both Bryan Ferry and Bryan Adams on the same day at Knebworth.

www.hatingdating.com

A dating website for people who just can't be arsed with it all anymore and are resigned to being single. You register but then that's it. No need to check other profiles, send tentative emails or meet anyone. Extremely popular in the East Midlands and Canada.

www.trevorbooking.com

Book theatre, concert and film tickets online. 2% of all sales go towards funding a new home with a brook running through its garden, for ex-England footballer Trevor Brooking.

www.lukewarmmail.com

For people who like to receive their email a few days late.

www.youcantalk.com

A forum for hypocrites to criticise each other.

www.milkshakespeare.com

Purveyors of unusual milkshakes named after the works of William Shakespeare. Shakes include 'Fruitius Cheeser', 'Almondy and Brieopatra', 'The Mulberry & Chives of Windsor' and 'A Midsummer Sprite & Double Cream'.

E seven sharp nine.
(It's called the Hendrix chord.)
Ambiguous
For once major and minor fight
On equal terms.

Here it's OK to be flat,
To feel diminished,
To walk between the black notes,
To know this is somewhere richer.

JUST LIKE NOAH'S ARK

There's a place just down the street
Where all sorts of people meet
Shall I tell you how to find it
You know the bus stop – right behind it.

Handwritten sign above the stairs
'New members welcome' it declares
No card, no rules, no joining fee
Beer flowing all night till half past three.

Old jukebox glowing in the dark
The place is just like Noah's Ark
All kinds of people, two by two –
Two punks, two drunks, two businessmen,
two skinheads sniffing glue.

The drinking hours aren't displayed –
No point in asking for a raid
But I can tell you how to find it
You know the bus stop – past the bike shop –
the doorbell's right behind it.

lions

How sad it is
That our children
Have lost the ability
To track, and steal
Meat from lions

But how lucky
To be able
To find lion's meat
In the supermarket,
And with Nectar points

On first looking into the
oriental chill cabinet at Waitrose

Susie, roll the rice,
Form a mutant teenage Liquorice Allsort,
A distant runt-cousin of a Swiss roll.
Let's have it in black and white –
You see, I'm a stranger here myself.

Susie, roll me your sushi
Sharpen the blade
Perform the rite, just for me
Show me the eye of the cucumber
A little vinegar for my rice
A dream of ginger.

Taking off the lid
I discover your miscellaneous
Drug-baron like micro packages
The green plastic fern
The plastic fish that squirts soy sauce.

I wouldn't have bought you
If you hadn't been reduced
You cut-price Samurai,
A dream of skill and love
Swimming round the kitchen
A little fish out of water.

My materialism is held as
stubbornly as any sheep
Sticks to mountain ground.

ParadoX

If you don't believe me,
I'll come back to haunt you.

Cráy fishing

In autumn 2000, Alan Fraser took Nick and me crayfishing for the first time. This happened to coincide with the death of Reggie, the last of the infamous Kray brothers, gangsters who had terrorised East London.

An adventure at dusk by Pudlicote bridge
In a rising Evenlode mist
Humans and river crustaceans
In a traditional autumn tryst

Meshes of metal hung from a string
A pig heart wired to the grill
Bait for Ronnie and Reggie
Who would both be keen for the kill

Soft splash in swift-flowing stream
Then the trap sinks down to the mud
There's a wait that seems too long to bear
While the creatures sense the blood

As the grill's hauled up over forked stick
Dark scorpion shapes cling to the flesh
A fumbling attempt keeps them there
Until the bucket is under the mesh

Shaken off and imprisoned they scrabble around
Waving East End boxers' claws
Tangled feelers as long as themselves
And scavenging, gangster jaws

If there's nothing else, they'll eat each other
To all sense of morality numb
Primitive, but highly successful
And by reputation kind to their Mum

Back home in the boiling, salted pot
Their sludge colour changes to red
There's a quick, convulsive movement
Though we hope they're already dead

Sweet nuggets of flesh in the armoured tail
Are good, though nothing like lobster
But there's a scrap to be found in the pincers too,
And that's enough for a mobster.

The native crayfish, which is protected, is small and black. You are much more likely to find the introduced American species which is larger and has red claws.

The song of the instrument case

It's more of a physical thing,
Travelling companions,
Somewhat taken for granted
I take the hard knocks,
The gaze of strangers,
It's me who feels the weather.

Heavy and awkward,
A thing of straps and handles,
Volume beyond my weight.

I'm the homemaker,
the exoskeleton,
The coracle, the body-bag –
Hard on the outside,
Plushed and felted within.

I envy the way you touch her
The delicacy of her body
The patina of her skin
When she cries
Everybody listens.

Foreplay

There used to be romance in foreplay
Now it's a case of 'You show me your mammogram
And I'll show you my PSA'

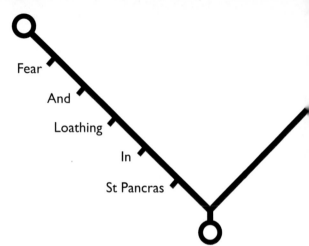

Fear
And
Loathing
In
St Pancras

I'm trying to ignore it but everywhere I look, there it is. The Government health ad; the panic-stricken headline on the front of the *Metro*; the mask-wearing oriental teenager; the coughing man; the spluttering woman.

I'm trapped underground on the Northern line, like mutton to the massacre. A wafer-thin drama student next to me is chatting to her friend, *'I've heard it can survive for up to two days on a tennis ball'*. I hate her for saying that, especially as Wimbledon has just started.

I scan the carriage for people holding programmes or sporting strawberry and cream stains on their tee-shirts. Thankfully, to my advantage, of that description there is no game, set and match. But I'm still anxious all the same. God, I wish I was slazengered right now.

The tube comes to a standstill in between stations. Always unnerving at the best of times. Cue an announcement from the driver: *'Ladies and Gentlemen, how is everyone feeling right now?'* It's a puzzling announcement. Why would the driver ask how we were all feeling, and, more sinisterly, what's with the 'right now' bit? 'Right now' implies an impending change to our situation – like an announcement preceding a roller coaster ride. If only there was a tube hostess to seek reassurance from – and perhaps a gin and tonic to calm the nerves. Another announcement from the driver, *'Sorry for the delay my beautiful ladies and gentleman but now we're up, up and away!'* Thank God. Nothing macabre. He's just a tad eccentric.

We stop at Camden Town. I contemplate my next move. Get off here or go as far as the Northern line terminates (Northampton? Carlisle?) and then hail a cab to take me to a low-populated island on the West Scottish coast whilst Bruce Willis or Samuel L Jackson is called in to wipe this damn thing from the earth.

I decide on getting out at Camden. I'm completely out of joss sticks and the risks of finding any on a low-populated Scottish island are just too high. Pandemic or no pandemic, a man's gotta have his joss sticks.

However, at the top of the escalators we are greeted by a makeshift sign:

DUE TO A COMBINATION OF THE PANDEMIC AND JOSS STICK SHORTAGES, CAMDEN TOWN IS CLOSED UNTIL FURTHER NOTICE. PLEASE CONTINUE ONWARD TO HIGH BARNET WHERE McCLUSKEYS TAXIS OF EIGG ISLAND WILL BE WAITING FOR YOU. WE APOLOGISE FOR THE INCONVENIENCE. IN SAMUEL L JACKSON WE TRUST. THANK YOU AND MIND THE GAP.

Fishing
FORECASTS

Fair Rose

Losing my identity

Veering, only moderate

I am the Minches merging with Hebrides

Utsire, **north**
and
south

Give me Tyne, Fast net,

Good visibility

Lundy, soul and Fair Isle

Or Ice land squalls

Hi Dogger

40s, and a Fisher

Losing her identity

IT'S DOVER,

German Blight, and Bailiff,

Ply mouth but malign head

Rock all!

But, on the   *It's Finis tear.*
h o r i z o n

The wind in the trees
The hum of the computer
A space for your breath.

Jack on the black, white, silver rock

Cuss them, Jack Boy!
Hang onto your shining bob
Say I see you, Mister,
Keep off my land.
⸰ You were the first, Jack
You worked the white tin
From the tinted, tainted rock,
Worked the hedge-wood to a plough,
Worked iron to the wheel.

You were the first
Hawking the green
At a brass halfpenny each
To the men with their clean hands out.
I work for my money, Mister,
Keep off my land.

Jack, I thank you for your colours,
But I know
Time changes a man's palette:
Complex earth shades become primaries,
Our landscapes do not fade
But lose their subtlety.

Times and colours are running, Jack,
Cuss them, Boy,
Hang onto those shining bobs,
Say: I see you, Mister,
Keep off my land!
Husband it for another day.

Teleph One

My sweet little telephone, curled up in the corner
I want to feel my lips on your cold smooth skin
Want to hold you close, feel my fingers upon you
Want to be beside you, want to hear you ring.

I only want to talk to you,
    don't want to play games with you
Sometimes you don't speak for days,
    sometimes you never stop
Sometimes I think you're your own worst enemy
Sometimes I take you off the hook
    when I go out to the shop.

My sweet old-fashioned telephone,
    curled up in the corner
I want to hold you in my hand and show you I care
You know I'll drop everything,
    the moment I hear you ring
I know I can call on you – you'll always be there.

She held her comic,

A small

Drawn, etched, coloured, chosen, loved,

princess

Like a steel sword guard

falling

Against the blows of the night.

asleep

The fine lines protected her.

It's all in the census

'For we should not forget the ordering of things'

I

Lord Palmerston,

Like the Emperor Augustus, sent registrars.

They came to Hay-on-Wye in 1861.

Along the road to Brecon,

Beyond the almshouse, knocking

At each small cottage door,

They find in Royal Oak Row

A seamstress, Elizabeth,

Perhaps named for John the Baptist's Mam.

Far from barren, she'd had four sons

By Henry, coachman, who died a while ago.

But there's also Alfred, born in 1852,

When she was long a widow.

If, in the desire above all to be exact,

An abrupt line ruled on a certificate

Is all the evidence of what his father's name might be,

Do you draw a blank on history?

II

In 1891, Great-Great Uncle Henry,
The second with that mark,
Was porter in a Wiltshire workhouse.
Born more than fifty years before
In Breconshire,
He'd had his fill as clerk.

The workhouse nurse was Rachel Spittle.
Among inmates, a Francis Cackhead's on the census list.
Less fittingly,
All those classified as 'imbecile' are Smiths.

III

The winds off Hay Bluff
Blew other Stepneys south and east.
Among them the Alfred with no acknowledged Dad.
A grocer, who now choses to be called George,
He marries Emma Gowing in Trevethin.
At the wedding, his father is recorded as deceased.

In 1878, their first surviving son
(The previous one stillborn)
Is given as his Christian names: George Alfred Shipton.
So, might the "George" and "Shipton" be
The record of his true paternity?

IV

Two branches down the line,
Eva, Nick and Trystan,
Grafted onto Russian-Polish stock,
Are the latest offshoots of the family tree.
But, close to its root, remains
A small and not unwelcome knot of mystery.

Pasteur Noster

By the end of the nineteenth century the pasteurisation of milk in this country was widespread. However, one farmer from the South West of England believed religiously in providing pure, untreated milk.

Our Farmer, who art in Devon

Harold Webb be thy name

Thy cows will come

Milking will be done

As it was back in 1307

Give us this day

What Daisy was fed

And forgive us our non-pasteurising

As we forgive them that non-pasteurised before us

And lead us not into the temptation of UHT

To deliver unto dairies

For thy will bring to them

The power, and the glory

Of rawer and rawer milk

Amen.

Labour Report

(and bits about potatoes)

Saturday morning. Wet. The pregnant seed
potatoes make it from the damp plastic
carrier bag to the egg trays in the new
baby's room. (The variety: Epicure.) This is
almost spring!

In the greengrocer's that morning everyone
seemed to know that you had had a show.
Their potatoes promise little – it's been a
bad year for potatoes.

You twinge. A gobbled lunch of simple
food (no potatoes – they deserve lots of
time). We couldn't find the pink book
– the one that tells you when to go to the
hospital. Eventually you find it under
knitting-patterns.

We drive to the hospital in my brother's
car. He's on holiday in France. I wonder
which potato varieties they grow there.
We find a parking place. (I was worried we
wouldn't and would have to go back home.)

The seismograph records your belly-quakes
– could it really be you'll be another sumo

wrestler out of a job? I mark Third Year exam papers.
You have a feminist novel. I read *Midnight's Children*.
Television. Peasants in France. Peter Maxwell Davies
talks about his Third Symphony. A woman wanders by,
listens keenly. I don't think the music connects.
She telephones.

Another room. Something is happening. You don't
want me to laugh. Our breath starts the long
slow double concerto. Should we tell Max? We go
downstairs. It's just after midnight and cleaners and
porters and tea-makers are abroad. We meet our
midwife. We were almost neighbours. I almost knew
her husband. We like her. She wears a chain of the
thinnest gold. No crucifix. A second movement to our
double concerto. The theme, no common riff this, is
stated, amplified, elaborated, and restated. It grows
in intensity. The midwife conducts a little but gives
the soloist room to explore. I play second fiddle. Time
after time. You go *sforzando fff* . The soloist plays her
cadenza. Your perineum swells like a massive orange.
The baby is there. It's a boy.

The sumo wrestler is gone. Your stomach is like an old
potato. So it goes. A new contestant steps into the ring.
New music.

IN PRAISE OF

FRICTION

It makes the wheels go round,
While things go in and out.
And so the race continues.

w^{MAKE A}ish

I wish I could get up
With the morning dew
Instead I lie, until it's dry
Even if that's half past two

I wish I could enjoy Abba at weddings
The post vol-au-vent voulez-vous
I wish I was comfortable with wedding conversation,
'So, how do you know Mike and Laura?'
And 'So, what is it that you do?'

I wish I could win at Trivial Pursuit
I always need a green, yellow, brown and blue
I wish I could finish crosswords
But I haven't got a clue

I wish I was quicker at RSVPs
Or asking back for an IOU
I wish I wasn't shy of DIY
And that my ASAPs were true

PTO

I wish I could remember names
Was it Sonia, Sophie or Sue?
I think it was Sue
But I'll wait until someone else says it first
Then casually say it myself, like I really knew

I wish I could sit happily in a pub when I can't have booze
I wish I understood what they said in the News
I wish I could be myself when I'm talking in queues
I wish I could use cutlery that's already been used

I wish I could paint like Monet
Or draw like Leonardo drew
Or at least like John Hubley
Who created Mr Magoo

I wish I wasn't so self-conscious talking to babies
In that high-pitched voice their parents do
I wish I was a master of all accents
And not just the Scotsman from Kathmandu

But ... as for ending wishful poems
With a profound point of view ...

... well, yes, I must confess
I wish I could do that too.

How to make a stranger laugh

An excerpt from www.liberatingfridays.blogspot.co.uk

On a walk to the Stag at Offchurch, a woman passed me walking four dogs, spectacular in their variety. I stopped and complimented the woman on her 'nice array'. She laughed out loud.

I could have just said 'Hi' but with a little extra thought and effort I've upped her endorphins and given her something amusing to share when she gets back home to the husband: 'Keith, I was walking earlier near Offchurch and this jolly man passed by, looking at the dogs. He turned to me and said 'nice array'. Oh Keith how I laughed. I mean it's what you say about flowers isn't it Keith. Not dogs.'

B**SUPPERTIME**lues

I guess I have a reputation for enjoying the finer things in life – fast cars, beautiful women, expensive clothes, but it's really my knowledge of fine wine that separates me from the rest of the crowd. So when a young lady was having a little difficulty at my local Co-operative Society supermarket, well I just had to help.

She said I'm looking for a Red that will work with fish.
She said I'm looking for a Red that will work with fish.
I said I'm a commis-chef and you're my kind of dish.

I'm as shy as a coconut and, Baby you knock me out.
I'm as shy as a coconut and, Baby you knock me out.
Come on over for supper and I don't mean Sauerkraut.

She said Can you sauter?
I said I'll jump for you the live-long day.
She said Can you sauter?
I said I'll jump for you the live-long day.
Sheesh!
You got me skewered like a holy man who's lost his way.

I believe in cod, vinegar, chips and peas.
I believe in cod, vinegar, chips and peas.
I believe in kisses that taste just like the sea.

I said I'm a backwoodsman. She said I like your stile.
I said I'm a backwoodsman. She said I like your stile.
Come on in my kitchen, I'm getting hungry, honey-chile.

I'll love you, Baby, the way I love rock and roll.
I'll love you, Baby, the way I love rock and roll.
Till they lay me on that slab and fillet my Jelly-Roll Sole.

A Show of
HANDS

People often tell me
I've got too much time on my hands

But I always say to them

'Better to have too much time on your
hands than too many hands on your time'

The boss's hands

The bank manager's hands

The mortgage lender's hands

The car salesman's hands

The insurer's hands

The travel agent's hands

The lottery ticket seller's hands

The director general of the BBC's hands

I mean, I could go on

But I really don't have the time.

The wood's grain
The waves of the sea
A new boat.

Two

Swifts scythe and chatter in the cooling air
On the posh house next door
Japanese air con strutted to the wall
A fresh black BMW dominates the garden
Its silver grill bared like fangs.

gardens

Where I am, an untended but graceful apple tree
Stray trails of vine
An old stone barn, lintel boughs bowed
And a ladder to the loft
Not a single step square against the uprights
And each a different length
A wonky piece of work, even by my standards

I'd trust my life to the BMW
But not to the ladder
And yet I like it more.

Slovenia, August 2012

WHAT THE MENUKI SAID

Hiding inside your hand
Knowing your fingers better than you do
Always there
Tightly bound

I know you don't want to lose me
It's only you who comes close
It's only you who touches
I am why you fight.

Wet dog in the rain

After the News at Ten, and all-important local weather,
A click of fingers brings him running to the open door.
Best keep him on the tether
Since a rippling nose suggests the whiff of deer.
He deserves this day's last chance
Of meting urine out in little sprinkles
Compulsively to assert his presence
By pissing on the world's abundant walls and wrinkles.

But, not understanding the essence of a depression
He does not realise that in this evening's rain
The heavens will piss on him.
His mark diluted so that it is pissed in vain

Happier to have a piss in sun
Eloquently adding to a much-frequented wall
A visitors' book at every corner
More pungent than a pub urinal
A track of each dog's wanderings in space and time
Informative of age, sex and infirmity
I too passed here and more recently
Than you.

Festiva<inline style="vertical">WILDERNESS 2012</inline>
message board

Hi Bill and Kathy, I've dumped my bags
By the tent with the giant foxglove flags

Now I'm in three minds about what to do next –
Suggestions please by Post-it or text

You can carve a block of Portland stone

Strike out in the forest on your own

Support the school with tea and cake

Go for a swim in the secret lake

Or translate some racy Latin verse
And contemplate the universe

SATURDAY

This morning I think I love you all
(Blame it on last night's masked ball)

A kid just beat me at ping-pong

I've got a new all-time favourite song

I met a girl from San Francisco
Then lost her at the roller-disco

I'm stuck with these temporary tattoos

This way to the portaloos

Help me please – I've lost my tent!

Did you see which way it went?

I think it's time we named the streets
(These Post-its have less space than tweets)

Today I think I'm nil by mouth

    Tonight is anyone heading back south?

Free to good home – case of apricot wine
(It seemed like a good idea at the time)

    How come I've got so much stuff to shift?

And I still really need a lift!

    Who's got a thing for men in kilts?

I've ended up with two left stilts

    Doesn't anyone live around Sidcup?

I'm sorry, mate – our car's full up!

    But my boss will kill me if I'm late …

So why go back to a job you hate?

Now Monday morning's come and gone
I've jacked my job and I'm staying on

What happens next is fine with me …
There's nowhere that I'd rather be.

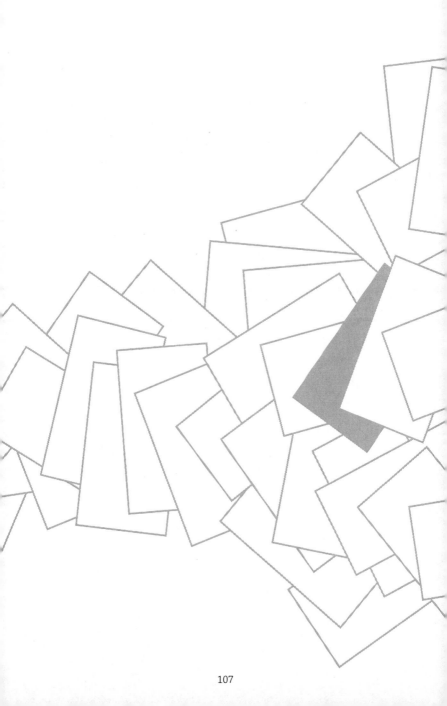

ON A FOOTBALL FIELD IN ESSEX: OUR TEAM VS ANOTHER TEAM

The opposition were 'orrible, hackers to a man. Fat-gutted tossers with the ball.

Yobbos to the last of 'em. With no soccer skills at all.

The only plan they could contrive
Was boot the ball and trust to luck
Anyone on our team was called 'a silly fuck'.
With play fouler than their effing mouths,
With trip, and barge, shove in the back,
They countered our subtler art
And smothered any promising attack.

But with a full time score of four to four
The shoot-out of sudden death would play its part
Our goalie saved with courage well beyond his years
Diving left, then right with almost clairvoyant flair;
And our penalties too were finely judged
To bring a victory that was fair.

And what, you may ask, abaht the bleeding ref?
Well throughout he'd seemed miraculously struck
Both blind and doorpost deaf
So if from this mock heroic tale
A moral you seek to draw
It's not the bleeding refs but poets
Who truly see the score.

How to spend a lottery win of **£29,016.66**

Incremental payments of £100, £200, £400, £800, £1500, £5000 and £10,000	on a running track
£2001	on DVDs of films set in space
£1966	on goal-line technology
£1812	on an old cannon, some cannon balls, a load of fireworks and a Tchaikovsky CD
£1000	on a grand piano
£999	on emergency items
£666	on a rare 7" pressing of the Rolling Stones 'Sympathy for the Devil'
£500	sponsoring a charity walk by the Scottish band, the Proclaimers
£500 more	sponsoring a charity walk by the Scottish band, the Proclaimers
£366	on leap-year calendars

£321 on a dusty bin

£180 on a dartboard

£147 on a weekend break to a
snooker-themed resort

£101 on filling up a room with snakes, dentists,
rats, needles, Dracula, insurance policies,
spiders, LSD, pterodactyls, Hitler,
cockroaches, ventriloquist's puppets,
sharks, appendicitis, asbestos, ghosts,
extremely high and narrow bridges,
Davros the leader of the Daleks,
Daleks and Heinz sandwich spread

£99 on red balloons

£88 on dinner with two fat ladies

£69 on a signed copy of the Karma Sutra

£65 on a carriage clock or a set of golf clubs

£40 on day wear

£40 on night wear

£18 on a certificate

£15 on another certificate

£13 on a Lucky Dip

£10.66 on a bus ticket to Hastings.

Colouring in literature

She bestows the Day-Glo,
Luminous acid-green for character,
Fluorescent baby-pink for plot,
Safety-jacket yellow for irony.

1

These are the important bits,
Workmanlike,
Like colouring counties,
rainfall distribution,
Oil deposits.

2

This is Act One.

3

Colouring Key: 1 Larkin's Blue   **2** Eliot's Grey   **3** Heaney's Green
4 Orwell's Red   **5** Auden's Pink   **6** Walker's Purple

4

Compare and contrast
The toddler's disrespect for boundaries,
Fat crayons in tiny hands
Cross the thick black lines
Of cheap and cheerful colouring books.

5

I want to respect her.
It's nostalgia
For the first meeting with a text,
Something with something to say,
For being 17.

6

The Highlighter Pen –
The beginning of Postmodernism – Discuss
City blocks of colour
Over tenant words,
Uncompromising urban renewal,
Double-glazing,
Instant lawns.

Young and pretty,
She's written her name in the front.
Easy with literature.
Why didn't someone tell me?
(Unreasonable, unbiddable toddler)
This is how it's done.

O

Charlbury
fish
van
___

Charlbury
fish
van
___

where
fore
art
thou
___

Charlbury
fish
van

A poem based on true events

For six long years I've trawled
the chartered streets of Charlbury
Driven on by hearsay,
gossip and Chinese whispers
I've hunted fresh halibut,
scallops and kippers

I've frequented pubs
The playground of the rumour
But talk there was of
speed humps and cricket
Not mackerel and tuna

An informer from Crawborough
Told me his niece from Ticknell Piece
Had seen the van outside the Co-op
So there I hurried
But all I found
Was a tied-up hound
And a school of youths
in high-rise hoodies
and low-rise jeans
Not a sniff of cockles,
sea bass or langoustines

I chased up on further leads
Sightings of cod and haddock
in Wychwood Paddocks
Of jellied eels
on Nine Acres fields
Of salmon terrine
by The Green
And fillet of shark
near Cornbury Park
But alas ...
... they were all red herrings

Desperate, I dialled 118 118
Fishing for a number
But for 'Fish Vans in Charlbury'
Nothing came under
I googled, yahooed and even asked Jeeves
But links to a campsite in Swansea
Was all I received

Then it came to me ... of course
The clue was in the name
If the van would stop anywhere
It must be Fishers Lane ...

Over seven days and seven nights
I sat there through wind and rain
A resilient fisherman riding a storm
My catch would be worth my pain

But the only van that passed
Contained nothing from the seas
The only van to pass me
Was detecting for TVs

On a grey and chilly Tuesday, I abandoned ship
And with sorrows to drown
I shuffled myself forlornly
Towards the Rose and Crown

As I arrived the church bells chimed thrice
The sun appeared with one last roll of the dice
Shining down on a smiling man
Stood proudly behind a gleaming white van
And there, he bestowed
Upon my outstretched hands
A tail of monkfish
And a bag of clams.

We have * * many stars in Walcot

If a mantelpiece can be graced by a postcard

Caressed by Liz Hurley's lipsticked nipple (*)

Might the next thing be an artwork

Smudged by one of Shane Warne's balls?

*as attested by the Telegraph Magazine January 13th 2011

haiku & improvisation

JOHN [IN MEMORIAM] COLTRANE

Jumping from the head
Blue notes fall like silver leaves
The wild horse comes home
Blue head-notes
    Jumping
    Silver horses, leaving home
        This is the head-wind
           The hurricane
Silver head, blue head
Wild head
    Jumping, pushing, falling
    Horse head
        It's autumn in New York

Head wild, horse wild
   Silver wild
Leaves like notes
   Scrawled
At night-fall
At note-fall
   Jump-blues, home-blues
      Love blues
         Blues falling
      With a feeling
            Like rain, the silver rain
            The wild rain
         Coming home, coming home
Crying home
      Riding the wild horse
   Riding the leaves
         Flying home
The wild horse comes home
         Blue notes *fall*
                like
                  silver   *leaves*

About
Blue

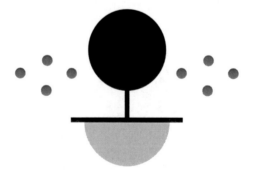

Imagine someone stopped me in the street
And asked, ever so politely,
'Do you own a dog?'

Even if he were hard at my heels,
Obedient as leather on the leash,
I'd probably say *'No'*.

Partly through pressure to be otherwise,
Not being with a dog is deep ingrained
In my identity.

But there are other times,
At the school gate,
Or on top of Brecon's Beacons –
After near three thousand feet of solid schlep –
When I see other dogs

And think they don't have half the heart,
Or pleasing symmetry of black and white,
Or lop-eared look of inquisition,
Or the sweet incongruity of
One eye brown and one eye blue

Of our dog.

Is there a book inside **me**

They say everybody has a book inside them
So I went to my local hospital for an X-ray
To see if it was true
It wasn't.
I had a heart, lungs and kidneys
But no book.

My hopes had been temporarily raised
When the radiologist found my appendix
But it wasn't that kind of appendix.

I was disappointed.
Sebastian Faulks, Delia Smith, Alan Shearer
All had books inside them
Why haven't I?

Desperate, I returned to hospital to have one put in.

My hardback lay on the operating table
My contents to be opened up
Foreword came the scalpel
An introduction made
Between skin and blade
But what followed was a sorry chapter.

The surgeon picked up the book
And about to proceed, he started to read
Engaged by every verb, adjective and noun
He just couldn't put it down
So he kept the book for himself
What I wanted in my body, now lives on his shelf.

In summary,
I am sentenced to accept
What I have inside me now,
I never will transcend

Last page

Final word

The End.

What's in a name?

ROB STEPNEY

An A to Z of poetry

Dangerous outside leaning

Walking the dog in winter

Browing old gracefully

When might time have
stopped?

It's a mistake to look in
the mirror

Arising from the Ashes

Beyond Newton's laws

I don't want to seem picky

Snow: Christmas in a Quaker
meeting house

Bad things were done
in Ephesus

Badminton

Gobble Devon dumpling

The miracle of flight

Not Adam's apple

Lesser spotted doxy

Lions

Paradox

Crayfishing

Foreplay

Fishing forecasts

It's all in the census

In praise of friction

Two gardens

Wet dog in the rain

On a football field in Essex

We have many stars in Walcot

About Blue

JOHN LANYON

From haiku tea 1/2/3/4/5
Curtains
Braggadocio
A good soldier
Happy birthday, love from Hazel
Swagbelly
Let's hear it for the weird kid
Casino of love
Touchstone
E7#9

On first looking into the
oriental chill cabinet at Waitrose
The song of the instrument case
Jack on the black, white,
silver rock
A small princess falling asleep
Labour report
Suppertime blues
What the menuki said
Colouring in literature
Haiku and improvisation
in memoriam John Coltrane

ADRIAN LANCINI

The first day of spring
Methyl mercaptan – what are you?
Coming out
The middle of nowhere
Our local
The dos and don'ts of leaving-dos
The man who wouldn't poo until
he got to work so he never had
to buy toilet paper
Hypothetical tribute acts –
a top 40

not com
Fear and loathing in St Pancras
Pasteur Noster
Make a wish
How to make a stranger laugh
A show of hands
How to spend a lottery win
of £29,016.66
O Charlbury fish van
Is there a book inside me?

EDWARD FENTON

Pierced
The towns and villages
of Oxfordshire
From Kite Hill
Dangerous men

Harpooning
Just like Noah's Ark
Sweet little telephone
Festival message board,
Wilderness 2012

ROB STEPNEY

It is wonderful to have found a delight in playing with language that is shared with Ed, John and Adrian; and it is exceptional that a small town such as Charlbury should contain so many other friends with whom to share the fun of poetry and performance. Colin and Richard Boddington were instrumental in the victory of 'our team' on a playing field in Essex, as I watched from the sidelines. Matti Aapro, who speaks most known languages, suggested I take the night train to Florence. Ian Richards introduced me to cricket at Edgbaston and is a constant companion. Several of the poems relate to Christina and our children Nick, Eva and Trystan. I am grateful for their love and patient encouragement: we have stars in Walcot.

ACKNOWLEDGE
MENTS

JOHN LANYON

Big thanks to Adrian, Ed and Rob for the care and imagination they have brought to this project; to Alan Fraser for believing in my lyrics and making the gigs happen; to the kingBs and Binliner Ensemble for performing my songs; to Keiko Tanaka for keeping me laughing and translating my haiku for Japanese readers; to Hazel, for the mystery; to Jack Rowe, Cornishman, and Arthur Smith who knows all the words to Swagbelly.

ADRIAN LANCINI

Hi Ed

Have you written an acknowledgement paragraph? Rob and John have. I'm not too fussed but may do a fictitious one. Your deadline is 11.59pm

Adrian

EDWARD FENTON

Hi Adrian

I thought about this after seeing Rob's, but honestly can't think of anything to say! I'm really glad that Rob invited me, but I've said that to him in person, and it wouldn't look good anyway to thank each other in the book. Deadline met!

Ed

Nothing on my back
Carrying the harvest moon
All the way home.